TEACH YOUR WIFE TO BE
A WIDOW

Teach Your Wife to Be a Widow

by Donald I. Rogers

Financial Editor, New York *Herald Tribune*

HENRY HOLT AND COMPANY • New York

Library of Congress Catalog Card Number: 53-5270

Printed in the United States of America

Dedicated to my wife,

MARJORIE

*Who patiently permitted me
to experiment with her time
and energy so that I might
learn how to go about
"teaching a wife to be a widow."*

FOREWORD

When a friend who was earning $20,000 a year was killed in a plane crash, my first thought, naturally, was of his widow. Calling to offer condolences, I was astounded to learn that she faced the imminent prospect of poverty. He had been in the process of changing his insurance program, had cashed in his old policies and had not taken out the new ones; he had left a staggering mortgage on their big, new home, which was not covered by mortgage insurance; he had invested unwisely and there was very little left in savings. With three small children, she faced a bleak future.

It set me thinking. Would my own wife, should she suddenly become a widow, be much better off? She knew little, if anything, about business affairs; she had no skills and aptitudes except those which go for making an excellent wife; she knew but few of my business and professional associates. How would she make out in the practical world of business?

My friend, the air crash victim, had depended on that good yearly income of his. While he was getting his $20,000, his mortgage wasn't "staggering" at all. Things were just fine. In fact, it was because of his success that he was changing his insurance program. Since, according to investigators of the air crash, he died without realizing that they were going to crack up, he at least went to his grave with a complacent mind.

I have given much thought to the problem he created and have related it to my own life, my own wife. The programs I have set down may not work for all who read this. They should work for most.

In the preparation of this book, I owe much to Mr. Robert A. Jones and Mr. Howard J. Carswell of the Guaranty Trust Company of New York; Mr. LeRoy B. Staver of the United States National Bank of Portland, Oregon; Mr. Thomas Staley, senior partner of Reynolds & Company, New York; Mrs. Gertrude E. Finn; Mr. Leon S. Theil; and, of course, my ever-lovin' wife, who held still for a vast amount of experimentation.

D. I. R.

East Hempstead, L. I.

CONTENTS

Chapter One

ℰℭℨℳℬ

ALL MY WORLDLY GOODS

There's a great deal of misunderstanding of the language of the marriage vow. A majority of husbands take too literally that phrase "until death do us part," and fail to comprehend the meaning of an equally significant and binding pledge: "With all my worldly goods, I thee endow."

That's the backbone of the contract, and this "until death do us part" business is no escape clause. Even after death, you're morally and legally committed to guard the welfare of the girl who signed the marriage license with you.

The American husband is a curious alloy of sentiment and ambition. He works harder than husbands in any other country of the world to "provide for the wife and kids" and then—in seven cases out of ten—passes to his reward before his wife does, leaving only an insurance policy and a mortgaged home.

Seldom is this enough to provide the skimpiest existence for his survivors.

To most young and middle-aged Americans, death does not seem inevitable. This attitude prevails even though more young people are killed by highway accidents and more middle-aged men are felled by heart attack in the United States than in any other country. "It can't happen to me," is the amazing outlook of the majority, and it results in only the most casual consideration of what will happen to the precious wife and kids once the family magnate has killed himself in the race against taxes and living costs.

The insurance peddlers have managed to wedge enough feet into enough doors to gain credence to the idea that the sojourn on this planet isn't permanent.

But insurance isn't enough, no matter how large the policy.

For years the insurance companies have been aware of the fact that an overwhelming majority of widows spend their lump-sum life insurance money within a year after receiving it. No one knows just how much insurance money is dissipated this way. The Institute of Life Insurance has tried to pin it down, without success. Some statisticians figure it's around 80 per cent, in other words, that $8 out of every $10 paid on the lives of husbands is gone before the first anniversary of his death rolls around, but the Institute of Life Insurance thinks that's a high estimate.

The fact is, the best wives often make the poorest

widows. Doting American husbands fail to realize it.

It's a rare wife, indeed, who knows all that can be known about her husband's business life, his income, his investments, his debts, and the way he handles his budget. Yet in this day of high speed on the highways and high pressure in the office, she may have the whole problem dumped on her lap without an hour's notice.

To the average wife, widowhood presents seemingly insurmountable obstacles and horrifying responsibilities, right at a time when she is least capable of dealing with them. It's not at all morbid—rather, it's only being sensible and kind—for a husband to spend years teaching his wife to be a widow. The odds are with the wife; he's more likely to die first.

How contrary the human mind! Not until the joints begin to creak do most men begin to think about what will happen to their wives if they die. But a man of 30 should be more concerned about his wife's widowhood than a man of 60. If a 30-year-old man dies, his wife (providing she's also thirty) faces up to 40 years of widowhood. When a couple is 60, things are much easier on a widow. She doesn't have to make the insurance money stretch so far; usually the house is paid for; the children are grown and perhaps can offer her a home if necessary. She has less need for a full education on how to be a widow than the girl with a home to pay for, a family to raise, and a husbandless future.

Which brings to point the most important thing for a husband and wife to realize about widowhood: there will be less money for a woman as a widow than there was when she was a wife. This simple and logical fact is rarely faced squarely.

How smug are the husbands when they get the wife and kids set up in a fine home surrounded by the good things money can buy. Yessir, they'll tell you, if anything happens to me, *my* family will be well fixed. It seldom occurs to them that with the husband's income cut off the mortgage payments alone would deplete all the money left by insurance and elsewhere in the estate in a comparatively short time.

The same men who out-fox business associates every day and who are known for their business acumen are the very ones who most frequently neglect to plan for their wives' welfare.

A friend of mine, a veritable wizard at his business, told me he felt very comfortable about his wife's chances of getting along if anything happened to him. She was a secretary before they married, he pointed out, and she could earn her living again if necessary.

I knew a good deal about this family and felt it my duty to point out some unalterable facts. They have been married 15 years and during that entire time the wife has never so much as typed a letter to a friend. Moreover, they have three children, the oldest 11 years old, all of whom require care. They live in a $25,000 home (pre-Korean value) in a fashionable suburb. The mortgage payments come to nearly $200 a month.

A highly skilled secretary in New York can earn something in the neighborhood of $70 a week. That's what my friend's wife would get if she were widowed and forced to go to work. We are, of course, over-looking the fact that she's rusty at her trade and that a great many younger and more proficient gals have come along since she tossed away her Gregg short-hand book.

But let's suppose she was lucky and landed a $70-a-week job. Fifty dollars would have to go toward the mortgage. (It's $200 a month.) There would be commutation fares and lunches to buy. And if she worked she'd have to pay someone to look after the children. It just wouldn't come out even. She'd be losing money.

The sole value of her secretarial background would be in supplementing the income her husband could arrange to leave for her. And she had better make it part-time employment, too, so she wouldn't be paying most of her income to a nursemaid for the children.

There's no reason why her husband shouldn't have realized these truths. People just hate to think that they'll die someday and thus they hate to make any post-mortem plans.

I told my friend it would be wise if they planned, together, how to handle her possible widowhood. Throughout the years she could have kept her hand in secretarial work, just for the practice. Perhaps she could have been secretary to a church committee and taken down the minutes of the meetings in short-hand. Maybe she could have helped her husband with some of his correspondence.

Almost weekly there are pitiful examples of shortsightedness that come across my desk, the result of ignorance, negligence, or reluctance to face reality.

After the tragic Thanksgiving Eve wreck on the Long Island Rail-Road in 1950, I received several appeals for advice from bewildered and distraught widows. They had been the gay or complacent wives of successful New Yorkers until that one awful evening when they lost their husbands. Whether it was days or weeks later, ultimately they encountered a frightening problem: how could they continue to run their expensive suburban homes and maintain their families? Several called me believing that as business and financial editor of the New York *Herald Tribune*, I could advise them.

"Can you tell me," asked one, "where do I cash in these stocks my husband left me? Do I go to the Stock Exchange?"

"All you have to do," I told her, "is call your broker."

"Any broker?"

"Well, no. The broker who sold them to your husband."

"But I don't know any broker. I don't know where he bought these stocks."

It developed the securities were shares of a Canadian company and had, apparently, been issued through a Canadian exchange. All I could suggest was that she contact any broker, let him prove the validity of the stocks by writing to the corporation, giving the serial numbers. Then the stocks could be traced through the underwriters to the broker who kept her husband's account. But the process could—

and probably did—take weeks. The value of the stocks could change, perhaps for the better, perhaps not. At best she wouldn't have her cash right away.

Silly? It's not at all unusual. It happens every day.

How much easier it would have been for her if her husband had kept a file of vital information in the house on the chance that his wife unexpectedly might become a widow.

Those were bleak December days for the widows of the Long Island Rail-Road wreck. Another called with a question that must have been asked by a dozen women who were unprepared for the responsibilities so tragically and ruthlessly thrust upon them.

"I want to hire a lawyer to sue the railroad," she said. "Shall I sell my husband's stock so I can give the attorney a retainer?"

Nothing could have been more foolish, of course. The stocks themselves showed her ability to pay. She could use them to guarantee the fee. If the lawyer was insistent, she could put them up for collateral and take out a loan to meet the fee, or better yet, find a lawyer who was more trusting.

A third Long Island Rail-Road widow had even a more drastic proposition: she wanted to know if it would be wise to withdraw all her savings to pay a lawyer a fee so she could sue the railroad.

These are minor details. But it's the little things in business life that sneak up and destroy fortunes, ruin homes, deplete estates.

The fact that women outlive men means, irrevocably, that the women—not necessarily the meek—are inheriting the earth. A man is a plain fool who is willing to work himself to an untimely death for the sake of acquiring a little wealth, but who fails to instruct his wife and other survivors what to do with it. If it is to be dumped unceremoniously into the hands of a naïve and inexperienced wife, he has wasted his life and thrown away the basic motivation of his existence.

Let there be no mistaking the inexorable acquisition of wealth by women. The recent census of stock ownership conducted by the Brookings Institution at the behest of the New York Stock Exchange shows that there are very nearly as many women shareholders as there are men. The Brookings people found there are 3,260,000 men and 3,230,000 women shareholders—only 30,000 more men than women. Men own 1,763,000 shares and women 1,308,000 shares.

Of the 33,179,450 shares of stock of the nation's most widely owned corporation, American Telephone & Telegraph Company, 39.5 per cent was held at the end of 1951 by women, 25.1 by men, 18.1 per cent by trustees, corporations, or brokers, and 17.3 per cent by joint owners, usually husband-and-wife partnerships. Statistics show that it is the women who will live longer; thus, the stock held in joint ownership will one day belong to more women than men.

It's never too early to begin to teach a wife to be a widow. If the thought is repugnant, consider that you're teaching her to be self-sufficient—just in case you have prolonged illness or other incapacitation. An ideal time to undertake the business education of a wife is the day a bridegroom returns to work following the honeymoon.

He has an easy approach at that time. He can claim—and with considerable logic and justification —that he's just too busy chasing the elusive family bacon to handle such vexing details as bills, taxes, and budgets. He can suggest that the bride could do a much better job of taking care of the family business matters than he could.

It takes only moderate preparation. Put a portion of your pay into a joint checking account. Then, after instructing the wife on how to make out checks and keep accurate records, turn over to her all the business chores of running the household. Let her pay all the bills. Let her decide how best to balance the budget. Let her figure out how much insurance you can carry (and you should carry as much as you can afford).

Then there's one more, one very drastic step. Let her work out the income tax!

Whether it's a joint return or a single one or two individual returns, let the wife do the work on it. Let her keep track of deductible expenses during the year, let her chart the entire tax program for the family from one March 15th to the next.

In this way, she'll have to be acutely aware of your business, of your income, of your expenses, of your investments. With this simple expedient of making her share the responsibility, she will, through the years, acquire a fairly decent knowledge of the business world. It'll be only a short time before she's asking you why you allow $200 to lie idle in the checking account when it could be earning 2½ per cent at a savings bank or even more if it were properly invested. Women have a penchant for details that men seldom possess. Once she's inoculated with the business bug, she'll be the best business partner you ever had.

The husband who makes a business partner of his wife will be rewarded tenfold. The free time he gains by having her handle the bills and checks and taxes is insignificant compared to the peace of mind he will acquire. He'll know, once his wife is a capable business woman, that she can handle herself and her family alone if the need arises. He'll know that if she should come into a large sum of money—say the payment of her husband's insurance policy—she'll not be stampeded into squandering it but, instead, will use the money wisely, exercising experienced business acumen, sound judgment, and seasoned reasoning. In short, she'll be one of the few "well-fixed" widows, and not a worry to her relatives or, worse, a charge of the community.

Chapter Two

❦✕❧

WHY YOU NEED A WILL

A man who has labored long in the vineyard to acquire a modicum of security and surround himself with a few possessions, has the right—the moral *and* legal right—to say how his goods and chattels will be handled after he dies. The law gives him virtual carte blanche (within reason, of course) as to what he can do with his belongings.

There are cases on record where huge sums have been left to or for canaries, cats, tropical fish, casual acquaintances, foreign religious cults, and even to madams of unswank nocturnal establishments. So long as a man is of sound mind and knows what he's doing and does it willingly, he can usually assign his goods and money to whatever or whomever he pleases.

But no matter what he has to leave, be it only a couple of worn neckties and his favorite beer mug, a

21

man has the right to say what will become of his possessions after he dies.

If he has a wife and a family it is not just his right, it's his obligation to dispose of his worldly acquisitions by means of a will. It's obligatory on him to specify who will get his things.

It's a man's duty to his wife to name an executor of his estate who will help carry out the husband's last wishes to the wife's best advantage. Only with a will can a man be sure this will be accomplished.

He may want his wife to be executor of his estate. It is the practice in some states (notably those with laws derived from old Spanish law) to name a wife as administrator if no will is left. But in many states this is not so, and if there is no will specifically directing that the wife be appointed to handle the estate, there is no certainty that the surrogate or judge of probate will do so. Usually, however, she has the first crack at it by law.

It's an amazing commentary on American intelligence to realize that the vast majority of men who die each year do not leave wills. Yet a simple one costs only $10 or $15. For some reason, the practice of drawing wills seems to be confined to the rich or near-rich—the people who most frequently need a will the least. Common sense should tell a man that it's the widow of moderate means, whose husband leaves an estate of diminutive proportions, who most needs the clear, red-tape-cutting help of a will.

In many states it's absolutely necessary for a man who has children to leave a will if he wants to give all his money and property to his widow. If he doesn't have a will, she will usually get one third of the estate (depending on the state where they live) and the children will get two thirds.

It's true that if the children are minors, the widow can usually get herself appointed guardian or custodian of their inheritance, in the absence of a will, and thus can get control of the money. But imagine the difficulties a widow might have getting along on one third of her husband's estate while she waited for the probate court to give her permission to spend her children's money for their own necessities! If the children are adults, she does not get it at all.

Isn't it worth $10 or $15 to know that such difficulties can be avoided?

Surprisingly few men realize how rich they are. Middle-income wage and salary earners leave some fairly extensive estates. Unfortunately many of them die believing themselves poor men.

By the time he's 40, the average fellow has accumulated a great many possessions. He owns some real estate, a car, a house full of furniture, appliances, lawn tools and equipment, some workshop tools, sports equipment (don't forget the cost of those golf clubs), a decent wardrobe, and some hobby gadgets.

Add up the money invested in these items and it would feed and clothe a widow and her children for quite a while.

But unless all these things are left to a widow in a will, it might take special permission for her to sell the golf clubs, for instance, in order to pay the grocer.

It's the younger married couples who most need a will, though I do not imply that older couples can better get along without one.

Any lawyer will tell you that the bulk of applicants

for wills are middle-aged or older. Somehow young folks just never get around to thinking about such things as death and estates and taxes.

It's well known by most who will leave estates of substantial size that a will can be important in saving taxes. It's not so well recognized, however, that a will can save tax money on small and moderately sized estates, if a trust has been provided. For instance, a will can save estate taxes, in some cases, at the time of the property owner's death. It may minimize or avoid excessive future taxes in the estates of beneficiaries and, in many cases, may be the means of reducing family income taxes.

Here's why:

If property passes outright to a wife, it qualifies for a marital deduction up to 50 per cent of the adjusted gross estate. If there's no will, and if there are children, probably only one third of the property would thus pass outright to the wife. A good part of the marital deduction would be lost.

Then suppose both husband and wife own property and there is no will. Should the husband die, leaving his property to the wife, and then, should the wife die, the combined properties would be subject to an unnecessarily high tax when they pass to the wife's survivor. Suppose the wife's survivor is a son who has managed to acquire an estate of his own. Addition of the combined estates of his father and mother would present an estate tax problem of serious proportions. It could be eased with carefully prepared provisions in a will—or in this case, two wills, the father's and the mother's.

It should never be assumed, either, that the husband will die first and that he should be the only one to have a will. A mix-up sometimes occurs when property is jointly owned and neither husband nor wife has a will. It's true jointly owned property passes to the survivor without need for a will, but consideration should be given to what happens to the property upon death of the survivor. Joint owners should each have a will, just in case both should die together as in an automobile accident. Otherwise there could be delay in settlement of the estate while the court tried to decide who predeceased whom.

A will, then, is a plan. It's a man's plan for the welfare of his wife and children in the event of his death. It indicates he has given some thought to the well-being of his loved ones, and shows unmistakably whom he wants to act as executor of his estate, whom he wants to assemble and protect the assets he has worked so hard to accumulate, whom he wants to settle up his bills and shoulder the responsibilities he must relinquish.

There are many other compelling reasons why you should make a will.

Suppose you own nothing whatsoever. Suppose you're not even married, are just starting out in life with a minimum salary. You could get hit by a car on the way to work tomorrow morning. Your relatives, perhaps your parents, could claim that you had some life expectancy, some earning potential, and could sue the driver of the car. To whom do you want this money to go? Without a will your wishes are ignored, although specific distribution of such funds is provided by law in most states.

The most common problem arising from lack of a

will comes when a husband dies, leaving a house. He had supposed, obviously, that his wife would have the house. But after the husband's death, the widow finds that she cannot maintain the house, and needs to sell it. There are two small children. Under the law, the wife owns only one third of the house, the children the remainder. To sell it, the widow must have a special guardian appointed, and then get approval for the sale from the probate or orphan's court. This wife, in fact, can't touch more than one third of actual cash left by the husband, without getting court consent.

Since this book is directed primarily to husbands, let me give you the history of a friend of mine. He went up into New England, met a girl, and fell in love with her. He had pressed his attentions no more than a week when the girl's father ordered him off the property. The old man explained that since Jerry was of a different faith than Mary, he wouldn't allow the affair to progress further. If, he said, Jerry was to show up around there again, he'd have the law on him.

The inevitable happened. Mary communicated with Jerry secretly, and one day they eloped.

For 5 years Jerry and Mary were deliriously happy. But during the entire time, Mary's father remained coldly aloof. He wouldn't even answer their letters.

Jerry was successful in his advertising career. He bought a house and put it in Mary's name. He bought stocks and some government bonds and put them in Mary's name. He started a fairly decent savings account, in Mary's name.

Jerry never thought of a will for himself. He had already assigned everything to Mary. Like most husbands, the thought of a will for Mary never crossed his mind.

When Mary was stricken with polio, Jerry wired, then wrote, to her father. Even so, the old man never responded.

Mary's father never even showed up at her funeral.

He did show up with a lawyer, though, a couple of months after the funeral, claiming half Jerry's house, half his stocks and bonds, half the savings account. He had a right to them. Mary had not made a will. The old man, along with Jerry, shared in her estate. If he were a resident of New York State, Jerry could get $10,000 and half the residue of the estate, the remaining half going to Mary's father. If the estate were valued in New York at less than $10,000, Jerry would get it all.

In my own family, there's the story of a relative who separated from his wife and came back home to live with his sister. Before he died he piled up a fairly decent estate. As soon as his death was announced, the wife, whom he had not seen in 20 years, came to claim her share. She got half the estate by court order, while his sister, who had nursed him in sickness, cared for him in health, got a small settlement, there being other brothers and sisters who also shared in the remaining half.

Do you think *you* can get along without a will?

Chapter Three

THINGS TO CONSIDER IN A WILL

The best will is the simplest, though not necessarily the shortest. Lawyers' language is not wordy just because the legal lads become enthralled with the sound of their own typewriters. It's fulsome and oftentimes redundant because they want to be ultra careful. The professionals know that in order to provide for any contingencies they must be prepared. The ammunition of preparation in the legal trade is words. Legal language has been developing for many centuries; when lawyers use the word "residue" instead of "remainder," it is because they know that that word implies a definite meaning to other lawyers.

I will say at the outset that the only safe way to have a will drawn is by a competent lawyer. It's not a costly job; the small fee buys a great deal of peace of mind. In fact, when one considers how many wills do become bogged in legal difficulties, it's not worth the risk to have one prepared by an amateur.

Before he prepares his will or before he sees his lawyer, a man should consider first of all his bequests. Does he want all of his estate to go to his wife? Does he want any of it held in trust for his children? Does he want his wife to forfeit any of it in case she remarries? And who is to be executor of the will?

There is the question, too, often overlooked, of what he wants to do with his property if he and his wife die together, say, in an automobile accident. This, in turn, leads to the problem of guardianship of minor children and an alternate executor to step in and manage the estate.

It is not wise to have more than one signed copy of a will, though there is no objection to having as many unsigned copies as may be desired. If it is known, in some states, that more than one signed copy exists, the will cannot be probated until all known signed copies are presented.

It is not intended that after reading this chapter you can sit down at your typewriter, knock out a will, have it witnessed, and forget the whole matter. Because a will should be drawn to suit individual problems and situations, this chapter is designed to give you only some general ideas of what you should and should not do.

Only the most competent lawyer could set down a guide for the amateur in drawing a will, and then only after exhaustive research. While there's a thread of similarity running through the laws of all states, the details differ widely, particularly between those states whose laws were founded on the old English common law and those whose legal inheritance comes from the Spanish. So it's wisest, always, to consult a good lawyer in the state where one lives or is domiciled.

A word here about lawyers. They are not at all the sinister, crafty conspirators portrayed in fiction, movies, and television. By and large they're an ethical lot, upholding high professional standards as capably as doctors and dentists. Most lawyers do not charge exorbitant fees, though some get considerably more for their services than others. It's good to remember, though, that with lawyers, as with almost everything else, you generally get what you pay for. But that doesn't mean you shouldn't shop around. Competition is good for the practice of law, as it's good for anything else. The local bar association or legal aid society can always give a quick report on the reputation and capability of a lawyer, or can refer a person to one specializing in wills, trusts, and estates.

A certain frame of mind is helpful to the preparation of a will. Before he sees his lawyer, a man should ponder at length the disposition of his belongings. In old days, a will applied to real estate, while personal property was disposed of by testament. Today, a will disposes of both.

So, with the thought in mind that he's going to distribute everything he owns, both real and personal property, a man should approach his lawyer with a fairly well-formed plan.

There are some things that cannot be disposed of by will:

(1) Jointly owned property, owned by two persons with the right of survivorship, will pass by operation of the law to the surviving owner, no matter

what provision may be made in the deceased's will. The survivor becomes sole owner.

(2) Insurance policies, unless made payable to the man's "estate," cannot be touched by a will. If a man wants to change his beneficiary, he must make the change on his insurance policy, for no matter what he says in his will, it will have no effect.

(3) U. S. Savings Bonds, usually made out in the name of one person, payable on death to another, cannot be changed by terms of a will. They must pass to the person named on the bonds.

(4) Exempt property, set aside for a widow in most states, cannot be taken away by will. This small exemption is specifically earmarked for a widow and children and is not included in the estate for tax or accounting (inventory) purposes.

(5) Section 200 of the Surrogate Court Act of New York also provides that, among other things, one may not dispose of by will the family Bible, farm animals and enough food to care for them for sixty days, the family automobile, farm implements, and $1,000 in cash.

I would assume that anyone reading this book is not thinking of disinheritance—of cutting a wife or a husband out of the will. In most states, neither spouse may disinherit the other. Should a husband draw a will leaving nothing to his wife, she may invoke a "right of election" (and so may a surviving husband if his wife has cut him out of her will). This permits the surviving spouse to accept either the provisions of the will or a stated minimum share of the estate, usually the share that would have been inherited if there had been no will. In most states that would mean that a wife could collect at least one third.

In so-called Community Property states, it could mean she'd be entitled to one half.

Only in North Dakota and South Dakota may a wife disinherit her husband in respect to her real estate. She may disinherit him from her personal property only in Alaska, Delaware, Georgia, New Jersey, North Dakota, Oregon, Rhode Island, South Carolina, South Dakota, and Utah.

A husband may disinherit his wife of his real property in Alabama, Arizona, District of Columbia, Florida, Georgia, Michigan, North Carolina, North Dakota, South Carolina, South Dakota, Utah, and Wisconsin. He may disinherit her from his personal property in Alaska, Arizona, Delaware, Florida, Georgia, Michigan, New Jersey, North Carolina, North Dakota, Oregon, Rhode Island, South Carolina, South Dakota, Utah, and Wisconsin.

Thus, only in the two Dakotas is complete disinheritance allowed. And those are the only states without the right of election. In all the others there is a specified time limit within which the right of election must be exercised.

In the preparation of the will you will consider, of course, your wife's financial security as a widow. You will provide, according to the size of your estate and insurance program and securities, for the maximum comfort and minimum worry of the woman who has shared your life. You may instruct her, in your will, in the manner in which she is to provide for the children, though it is not possible to will her money with "strings on it." You can't give her, say, $10,000 to be used for Junior's education. It must be left in trust for Junior. In this connection, involving a third party, it is not possible to will your wife the money you *expect* to get from Uncle John's estate. If you die on June 1 and Uncle John dies on June 2, the money Uncle John left you goes to your estate and must be distributed as though there were no will. Uncle John, however, could eliminate any problem by setting up a trust and allowing you to dispose of, in your own will, any money that will eventually come to you via Uncle John's will and his trust.

When a man goes to his lawyer for the preparation of a will, he should consult him as a friend. Tell the lawyer everything about your life, your home, your finances, the success or failure of your marriage, your chances for business or professional success in the future. Lawyers are not called counselors through an accident in terms. That's their principal role—to counsel, to advise, to help. If you want, you can consider your lawyer as a paid professional friend who is bound by ethics and the standards of his calling to protect your confidences and act in your best interests.

He'll tell you what should go into a will, and will respect your wishes so far as possible in drawing it up. His main job will be to see that it's a binding document and has no legal loopholes that can knock your plans awry after you have died.

Once the will has been drawn he will show it to you, probably page by page. If there are any corrections or additions, the entire document must be re-typed. Not until it's in completed form, ready to be signed, will he fill in the date. When the whole document has your approval and you have indicated your desire to execute it, he will call in witnesses. The main restriction on witnesses is that they must not be named in the will as beneficiaries. Three witnesses are required in Connecticut, Georgia, Louisiana, Maine, Massachusetts, New Hampshire, the Philippines, Puerto Rico, South Carolina, and Vermont. All other states require at least two witnesses. It is a good idea to have as witnesses people who can be located easily; personally I favor as witnesses a lawyer and members of his staff.

He will ask you: "Is this your last will and testament? Do you wish to make any changes? Are you satisfied that, as now drawn, it expresses your will? Are you prepared to execute this will?"

Handing you the pen he will ask you to request the witnesses to witness your signature. You will then sign your name on the end of the will, and initial each page. Witnesses will make it official by signing their names and addresses.

As a final precaution, the lawyer will fasten the pages of the will together in such a way that they cannot be removed or even opened, without showing that they've been tampered with. This involves stapling machine, ribbon, or sealing wax, and sometimes all three. Then the will is inserted into an envelope and sealed, and you are asked to write your signature across the envelope and flap (again, so that it will show if the will is opened). The lawyers call this "the little drama."

It can be seen here why there should be no duplicate—at least no signed duplicate. In the event you sign more than one copy, all signed copies must be produced before the will can be probated, otherwise there is the presumption that you wanted the will revoked.

Yes, a will can be revoked, changed, or destroyed, despite the wide contrary belief. It's one of the advantages of a will over any other instrument. This doesn't become effective until you die.

You may revoke a will by a written statement, but this is a highly technical procedure and should be done only by a lawyer. A formal revocation is just as painstakingly executed as the will itself. Even a notarized statement of revocation cannot be accepted in many probate courts.

One way is to destroy your will. Certainly no will can be produced once you have destroyed it. But you may peer down from some astral vantage point to see that your survivors and former beneficiaries are proving in court that you did not destroy the will with *intent to revoke* and hence will get the terms of the will invoked by court decree. So the best way to revoke a will is to have your lawyer do it. He'll make the original null and void in the only safe way, by revoking it step by step in a separate document.

Storage of a will is important. It can be kept in a strong box, safe-deposit box, or a home safe. I have left mine in my lawyer's vault which, being fireproof and burglarproof, I considered the safest place. If a bank is named as executor or in a trust fund, the bank will hold the will in its safe-deposit box free of charge. Above all else, a will must not be moved about with too much frequency or with any amount of secrecy. You have a will drawn for one purpose only, to apportion out your property after death to those you want to benefit from it, so don't make finding your will a hazardous game of hide-'n'-seek. If it's not found, your good intentions may have been wasted. It may be recalled that the will disposing of Hetty Green's $90 million estate was found by accident under a soap dish in her house.

If the will is to be kept in a strong box or home safe, or even in a safe-deposit box, it's wise to attach a note with a paper clip. In bold letters state: **"Caution: Do Not Open: This Is an Original Will: Any Alteration or Tampering May Void the Will."**

To give you an idea of what goes into a simple will (and certainly *not* to serve as a guide in drawing your own), I print herewith a representative sample:

I, Sam P. Samuels, now residing at 667 Fisher Avenue, East Hempstead, New York, being of sound and disposing mind and memory do hereby make, publish, and declare the following as and for my Last Will and Testament, that is to say:

ARTICLE FIRST

I hereby revoke any and all wills and codicils thereto by me at any time heretofore made.

ARTICLE SECOND

I direct the payment by my Executrix of all my just debts and funeral expenses as soon after my decease as may be practicable.

ARTICLE THIRD

I have complete confidence that my wife MARJORIE R. SAMUELS will adequately provide for the education, maintenance, and support of my children, MARILYN L. SAMUELS, DONALD I. SAMUELS, and MARK N. SAMUELS, and I make no bequest to them, or any of them, on that account, nor to any other child or children who may be born to me after the effective date of this my will.

ARTICLE FOURTH

All the rest, residue, and remainder of my estate whether real, personal, or mixed, of which I may die seized or possessed, or to which I or my estate may be equitably entitled, I give, devise, and bequeath absolutely to my wife MARJORIE R. SAMUELS.

ARTICLE FIFTH

In the event my said wife shall predecease me, or die under circumstances which render it impossible or difficult to determine who predeceased the other, then I give, devise, and bequeath my residuary estate in equal shares to my said children,

MARILYN L. SAMUELS, DONALD I. SAM-
UELS, and MARK N. SAMUELS.

ARTICLE SIXTH

I nominate, constitute, and appoint as Executrix of
this my Last Will and Testament my said wife
MARJORIE R. SAMUELS, and direct that she
shall not be required to furnish any bond or other
security in order to qualify as such in any state or
jurisdiction.

In the event that my said wife shall predecease me or
die or fail for any reason to complete her duties as
such, then I nominate, constitute, and appoint as
Executrix of this my Last Will and Testament my
said daughter, MARILYN L. SAMUELS, if she is
not then a minor, or if she is then a minor, my
brother NORMAN E. SAMUELS, and I direct
that neither my said daughter nor my said brother
shall be required to furnish any bond or other
security in order to qualify as such in any state or
jurisdiction.

ARTICLE SEVENTH

I nominate, constitute, and appoint as Guardian of
the person and property of such of my children as
may be minors at the time of my death, my said
wife MARJORIE R. SAMUELS, and direct that
she shall not be required in order to qualify as
such, to give any bond or other security in any state
or jurisdiction.

If my said wife shall predecease me or die or become
incapacitated before my youngest child shall be-

come an adult then I nominate, constitute, and appoint as Guardian of the person and property of such of my children as may then be minors my said daughter, MARILYN L. SAMUELS, or if she is then still a minor, my said brother NORMAN E. SAMUELS, until and only until my said daughter shall become an adult, and I direct that neither my said daughter nor my said brother shall be required to furnish any bond or other security in order to qualify as such in any state or jurisdiction.

ARTICLE EIGHT

I authorize my Executrix to sell any real estate of which I may die seized or possessed and give good and valid conveyance therefor.

IN WITNESS WHEREOF, I have hereunto set my hand and affixed my seal this 30th day of April, in the year One thousand nine hundred and fifty-two.

Sam P. Samuels, (L.S.)

Marvin P. Hamilton
John S. Powers
Douglas Collins

On this 30th day of April, in the year One thousand nine hundred and fifty-two (1952) at 154 Nassau Street, New York City, the above named Testator, Sam P. Samuels, subscribed his name to the foregoing instrument and caused his seal to be thereto affixed in our sight and presence and at the same time declared to us and to each of us that the said instrument was his Last Will and Testament, and requested us and each of us to subscribe our names as witnesses thereto, which we now do in his sight and presence and in the sight and presence of each other after we have heard this attestation clause read aloud in the presence of the Testator and noted that it truly narrates the things that have been done as they occurred.

MARVIN P. HAMILTON
    Residing at 16017 33rd Avenue, Flushing, N. Y.
JOHN S. POWERS
    Residing at 224 Beach 138 St., Rockaway Beach, N. Y. C.
DOUGLAS COLLINS
    Residing at 19 Cypress St., Floral Park, N. Y.

There are two other forms of wills, one to be avoided, the other to be used in case of emergency. The first is the holographic will, or one written entirely in the handwriting of the testator (he's the one who's doing the bequeathing), and this type of will requires no witnesses. The second is the nuncupative will, or oral will.

An holographic will, or a will written in your own handwriting, is more frequently rejected than it is probated. A majority of states do not consider such a will valid. If you have one, take it to your lawyer and let him draw you a proper will. The only states and territories permitting holographic wills are Alaska, Arkansas, Arizona, California, Idaho, Kentucky, Louisiana, Mississippi, Montana, Nevada, North Carolina, North Dakota, Oklahoma, Puerto Rico, South Dakota, Tennessee, Texas, Utah, Virginia, West Virginia, and Wyoming.

Most states will recognize oral wills only if made by a soldier or sailor while in actual military service or by a mariner while at sea. There need not be immediate peril of death in order for the will to be uttered. At least two witnesses are necessary. There are, of course, rigid time limits on the validity of such a will.

One further thing to remember is that a will must be kept current as the size of the family changes or as your financial status changes.

Chapter Four

IT'S NOT *ALWAYS* SAFEST IN A BANK

If it were not for banks, we wouldn't have much of
an economy. Probably over 90 per cent of the homes
bought in any given year are paid for by mortgages
from banks or savings and loan associations. A lion's
share of business transactions are accomplished by
checks drawn on private banks.

Even so, even though banks daily perform wonder-
ful and cheap service for their customers and com-
munities, there is a startling ignorance of some of the
bank laws and some of the restrictions imposed on
bank services.

Upon the sudden death of a friend of mine, I
learned a bit about the ability of highly educated
people to misunderstand banking laws.

"We never had a joint checking account," his
widow said a day or two after the funeral, "but it's
all right because John always signed a whole book
full of checks."

She displayed a book of checks, all signed by John. The poor widow didn't know that the account was frozen the minute the bank learned of his death. No checks signed by John would be honored—even though they might have been drawn before his death.

This, in itself, results from the banks' desire to protect their customers. John was the customer, not his wife. A person who owns a checking account can always change his mind at the last minute and stop payment on a check. When his lips are sealed by death, the banks figure he isn't being given a fair chance to stop payment, so they refuse to honor any of his checks presented after they learn of his passing. A check is a revocable order to pay and death destroys that order.

More important an influence on this reasoning, however, is the angle of state taxes. Most states have inheritance taxes, though many estates aren't large enough to be hit by the federal tax. But a bank has no way of knowing how large an estate may be.

The money in a checking account must be listed in the assets of an estate and thus might be taxable. If there were no bank regulation to prohibit payment of checks of a dead man, a widow of unsavory scruples could write a check withdrawing all funds from the account, and in this way might avoid paying the estate tax.

It's not always easy for a bank to be adamant in such cases. One bank still salves an uneasy conscience over just such an incident.

A millionaire had enjoyed a long friendship with a doctor several years his junior. Throughout the years the doctor had treated the millionaire for many ailments and had never submitted a bill. On a Wednesday, the day before Thanksgiving, a few years ago, the millionaire called the doctor to the hotel where he lived.

"Fred," he said, "I certainly owe my life to you. You've saved it many times with your care and skill, and yet you've never sent a bill. I'm getting old and, as you know, I have no family. I'm a rich man and I want to do something for you. Here is an envelope. It contains my check for $100,000, made payable to you. Please take it as a token of the respect and gratitude I hold for you."

A short time later the doctor left, taking his check with him. He deposited it in his bank that afternoon. That night he drove to another town to spend the holiday with his family.

On Thanksgiving Day the old man died.

Next day, Friday, the check reached the bank on which it had been drawn. But that morning, bank officers had read the news of the millionaire's death. They refused to release the funds for the check.

The doctor hired counsel to find out why the $100,000 check of a man worth many times that should be held up.

The bankers were polite. They explained the regulation and suggested that he submit a bill for $100,000 to the old man's estate.

The doctor's lawyer saw a hazard there, though. "But that will be a bill for professional services and as such would be subject to income tax," he objected. "The old man wanted my client to have $100,000 and that's what he expects to get."

The bulk of the estate was left to a large university. After the school's board of directors had heard the tale, interviewed the doctor, had his story corroborated, and received an affidavit from the bank, they decided to make a gift of $100,000 to the physician, permitting him to have the money the old man wanted to give to him.

But it was a voluntary gift, given by an institution with no tax worries. The university had no legal obligation to give up the money.

Sometimes rules and regulations, which are drawn up to protect people against the hazards of the commercial world, work to the disadvantage of survivors and heirs.

This is true, in some states, in respect to joint checking and savings accounts. The regulations vary from state to state, but in some, the death of one or the other of the joint depositors results in immediate freezing of one half the account until taxes are settled.

This is a point to find out about in your own state. If you live in a place where your widow can withdraw quickly only half your account, perhaps you'd better enlarge the amount in the joint checking (or savings) account to tide her over the expensive and rough days she'd have if anything happened to you.

In this particular, and in those states where it applies, a bank protects a dead man better than it does a live one. If he's alive, his wife can withdraw all his savings, so long as she is joint owner of his account.

Some states where there is a state inheritance tax (as in New York) insist that banks seal a safe-deposit box upon the death of its renter. This applies even though the box is jointly owned by husband and wife. Soon as the bank learns of the death of one of the owners of a box it is sealed—literally sealed with a stamp and may not be opened until a state tax appraiser is present. This policy is followed frequently by banks in other states without inheritance taxes if it is known that the estate of the box holder is large enough to qualify for federal taxation.

When a well-known and colorful New York politician died at 10:30 one morning, some enterprising reporter got the story on the bank's news ticker within a half hour. A bank officer read the report in his downtown office, remembered that the gentleman and his wife had a joint safe-deposit box in a branch bank, and called the branch manager.

"Watch out for Helen So-and-So," he said. "I have just learned that Sam died. She may be at the safe-deposit box."

"Holy smoke!" cried the manager. "She just went down to the vaults now." He slammed down the phone and raced after Helen.

About 35 minutes had elapsed since Helen's husband had died, but she was already after his money. By the time the manager reached the vaults, Helen had opened the box and was stuffing papers and envelopes into her pocketbook under the patronizing scrutiny of a guard.

The manager signaled the guard to detain Helen, hurried back upstairs and to the street where he enlisted the assistance of a city policeman.

The manager and patrolman confronted Helen with the fact that she was violating a law.

Why for heaven's sake, said Helen, she had no idea it was against the law. Sam had died, she explained, and she wanted to see how things stood financially.

Be that as it may, the manager told her, everything must go back into the box.

Helen turned over a few papers.

The guard, who had witnessed the withdrawal, asked:

"What about that big brown envelope?"

"That's mine," Helen said. "That's not Sam's. It's an envelope Sam gave to me and I want it."

So the manager explained it again. The brown envelope—*everything*—had to go back into the box and it had to be sealed. If the envelope did, indeed, belong to Helen personally, she could have it eventually, after the representative from the tax commissioner's office had made an appraisal and after Helen proved it was hers.

Helen left in a cloudburst of invectives, threatening to get her lawyer.

Trying to help Helen as much as possible, the bank manager arranged for the tax man to be there the following morning. Helen came, attended by her counsel.

The papers Helen had surrendered willingly included insurance policies, deeds, and other legal instruments. The brown envelope was broken open and revealed $10,000, all in $1,000 bills.

Helen restated her claim. Sam had given that money to her, she said, and it should not be considered part of his estate. But there was nothing on the envelope or in it to indicate it was Helen's and not Sam's. If it indicated anything to the tax man, it was that Sam had received a windfall he didn't want recorded in his checking or savings account.

Nevertheless, Helen sued. She produced an old timer who formerly worked with Sam years before. The witness said that he distinctly recalled that Sam had told him he was going to give $10,000 to Helen and that he was going to put ten $1,000 bills in a brown envelope and place the envelope in their jointly owned safe-deposit box.

Nearly everyone connected with the case, the judge included, suspected the old man of lying, but there was no refuting the evidence; nothing would shake his testimony. Helen got her $10,000.

For all this, a safe-deposit box is a good thing to own. It's an ideally safe place for important papers such as insurance policies, deeds, your will, your birth certificate, and receipts you may need.

But one thing to remember about keeping insurance policies in a safe-deposit box. In order to collect insurance, it's necessary to surrender the policy. It will take a few days for the company to make the payment, so there's usually time enough to retrieve the policies from the deposit box. However, it's a good idea to have policy records at home: name of the insurance company, amount of the policy, its number, date of execution, and beneficiary.

Chapter Five

WILL SHE GET A HOME—
OR A MORTGAGE?

Some of the most aggressive businessmen in any community are those who sell insurance. With their enthusiasm for sales, their stiffening competition for the dwindling dollars, and their occasional less-than-ethical foot-in-the-door tactics, they have, nevertheless, spread the good word. If any American is not aware of the fact that he *can* provide for his widow's security in a very painless and inexpensive manner, it's because he hasn't listened to some plain-talking insurance salesmen.

It's not my intention to present a case for the insurance companies. I don't feel that it's necessary.

I do think, however, that there is a great amount of misunderstanding about insurance plans and programs. Some people get talked into buying insurance programs they don't need; others refuse to listen to proposals that would serve them well and faithfully.

The companies have worked out myriad programs. All of them have to be fair and equitable plans or they wouldn't be approved by the various State Insurance Commissions.

In its simplest form, a life insurance program is a guarantee for you (or your survivor) in exchange for an investment on the part of the insurance companies. The companies guarantee to pay your survivor a stipulated sum when you die. In return you give them a certain amount of money each month or quarter or year. One individual may pay only a few dollars before he dies. Another may go on paying for years. The companies have figured it out "actuarially," which means that they know that a certain percentage of people will die at a certain age. All the figures are calculated when they determine how much you'll pay each month or quarter or year.

The companies have figured it out so that they don't lose. If one hapless chap takes out a policy for $10,000 and pays only $250 for his first year's premiums, then gets killed by a truck, obviously the company that sold him the policy has lost money. But you'll find that at the end of 20 years, or 40 or 50, the companies have earned a substantial amount of money. Of this there is no denying; Metropolitan and Prudential are two of the wealthiest enterprises in the republic. Neither of these is a profit-making concern for shareholders. All profits accrue to the benefit of policyholders.

What of the premiums you pay to the companies? They take them and invest them in stocks, bonds, mortgages, real estate, and other ventures. By and large these, too, are good investments. Thus the insurance companies make money in two directions— one on sales, another on investments. This is not unique; most businesses of any substance are conducted in just this same manner.

It leads to the point, however, of why you should turn your money over to another so that he can invest it and make more money on it. Why not do it yourself?

The answer's obvious, of course. If you're paying $500 a year for the family's insurance program, you can't do much with an investment in stocks of $500. Furthermore, in exchange for the $500, you're probably getting as much as $25,000 insurance coverage for the members of the family.

So far, O.K.

But what about the cash to be paid to your widow if you die? Are you insured for $10,000? For $15,000? Is she going to know how to invest that much money if, through unfortunate circumstances, it is paid to her in the next year or so?

Keenly aware of the fact that a great deal of insurance money paid to widows is spent rapidly and unwisely, the insurance companies have worked out scores of different programs which call for staggered monthly or annual payments to beneficiaries.

In other words, instead of getting $15,000 cash, you can arrange it so that your wife gets, say, $200 a month for a specified length of time; or, a certain amount per month for life. You can arrange this in any amounts (if you're willing to pay the premiums, of course) and can have it tied in with her social security benefits.

These are good programs, of course, and needed by a great many families.

Personally, I won't need one. You see, I've taught my wife to be a widow.

To me it doesn't seem necessary to let the insurance company retain my $40,000, invest it, earn money on it, and then dole out a certain amount of cash each month to my wife.

Instead, I'm preparing Marge to handle investments. She is a "student" of the financial pages of the newspapers. She is a close observer of the changing business-economic scene. When the time comes she will, God willing, know what to do. More on this in the next chapter.

This is the reason why I'm concentrating on what they call "ordinary" life insurance. This is next to the cheapest insurance they sell. The very cheapest is "term" insurance; that is, you pay in a certain minimum amount periodically, but get no dividends and accumulate no "savings" or cash-surrender value. Ordinary life insurance gathers dividends along the way and piles up a definite savings account in the hands of the company.

Mine is double indemnity insurance. If I die a natural death, Marge will get $40,000, but if I'm killed in an accident or otherwise meet a violent end, she'll get $80,000.

It means, too, that I have no particular need for the more expensive "retirement" policy. When and if I get to retirement age, my ordinary policy will have something like $30,000 cash-surrender value. I'll cash it in, take my $30,000, and settle back to enjoy some relaxation. I'll put some aside, of course, for final expenses like doctor's bills and funeral costs. As a matter of fact, my policy provides that I can withdraw any amount I want from the cash balance, and leave as much as I want as active insurance. I may do that: withdraw, say, $25,000 and leave $5,000 for what the Yankees used to call "settling costs." If I'm in good health, that $5,000 in cash-surrender value will give me more than $5,000 insurance. It'll be figured out actuarially, and the company will give me a definite figure—say, $7,100. (This is just a guess.)

One can apply this theory of mine on ordinary life to almost anything that's now covered by insurance programs.

You can take out an ordinary policy to cover the extent of the mortgage on your home and as soon as your diminishing mortgage and your rising cash-surrender figures coincide, cash in the policy, pay off the mortgage, and hold a neighborhood cocktail party.

An ordinary policy on my own life can guarantee an education for my sons. If I die, they'll have the full amount of the policy; if I don't, I can take the cash-surrender value when they reach college age.

The thing to remember about insurance is that you can make it work for you. Too many people become slaves to their premium payments, never fully realizing just what assets they possess in that formal, legal-looking document.

But the thing to remember about my own program with ordinary life insurance is that a wife must know how to handle large sums of money.

The alternative to having a lump sum payment given to a widow or having the proceeds paid out under regular settlement options, is to leave some of the insurance proceeds with the company at a guaranteed rate of interest, retaining for the beneficiary the unlimited right of withdrawal.

Like all good theorists, I'm inconsistent. While I know that I could work out a program of ordinary life coverage to handle the mortgage on my home, I have what the companies call a "mortgage redemption plan." Here's how it would work:

Let's suppose the mortgage on my home is $15,000. It is a mortgage which is reduced regularly by monthly payments to the bank.

The insurance company would give me a policy which, at the outset guarantees $15,139 on my life. In other words, if I died shortly after taking out the policy, that amount of money would have been given to the bank to pay off the mortgage, settle up interest charges, and pay the taxes. The guaranteed amount drops regularly with the reduced mortgage balance.

At the end of 20 years, I'll have left a life insurance policy of $5,700 and no mortgage. I can elect to do one of four things:

1. I can take a paid-up policy of $3,214, with no further payments;

2. I can extend the $5,700 of life insurance protection for 17 years without further premium payments;

3. I can receive $2,127.64 of guaranteed cash value plus about $1,213 in accumulated dividends; or,

4. I can continue the $5,700 of permanent life insurance protection at a reduced annual premium.

The regular annual premiums now are $201.44. I could continue the $5,700 of permanent life insurance protection for an annual premium of $158.40. If I do this, let the whole program go until I'm 65, I will have cash value plus accumulated dividends of $5,432.10, or I can take a monthly income of $32.85 for life, with payments of 10 years guaranteed.

Now, suppose I had taken a little risk, myself. Suppose I had figured I'd live a few years and could risk taking a $10,000 ordinary life policy to cover the $15,000 mortgage on my home. With double indemnity provisions, it would cost me about $225 a year. At the end of 20 years, my mortgage would be paid off, of course, and I'd have no need for the insurance. So I could cash in the policy. The cash-surrender value would be $3,320. Or I could let the policy ride on a "paid-up" basis, which would mean I'd have paid-up insurance without having to send in any more premium payments. Paid-up value at the end of 20 years would be $5,330.

But the thing to remember is that some time during that 20 years—I haven't the actuarial mind to figure it out—the amount of my mortgage and the cash-surrender value of my policy would coincide. The mortgage would be dropping, the cash-surrender value would be mounting. When they met, I could cash the policy and pay off the mortgage.

Any man's a fool to be without all the insurance

he can afford. It's good investment, sound planning, and the easiest way to build an estate.

The question revolves around how you want the benefits paid. If you believe you can really teach your wife to be a widow—to be a sound business manager —it's only sensible to get the money in a lump sum and let it work for her and earn additional dollars.

But if you feel she can't meet the requirements, then get staggered payments of the benefits. Just remember, you'll pay for the privilege: the premiums will be higher, *but your widow's money will be safe*.

Several things should come before an investment in securities or even before a savings account. A sound insurance program is one of the most important.

Chapter Six

GOOD INVESTMENTS FOR A WIDOW

No man in his right mind would let $10,000 lie idle without earning some interest. That's why it seems foolish to me when men make no provisions for the care and feeding of the money their widows will receive. There's hardly a man who doesn't have some sort of insurance program. Many have provided for monthly payments to their widows rather than for lump-sum settlements, but, as explained in the previous chapter, this may not be the wisest policy if a widow has been trained to handle money competently.

It's true that insurance companies pay some interest for the use of the money left in their possession when monthly payments are arranged for a beneficiary. But the interest doesn't approach the earnings that could be realized if the widow could exercise sound judgment and know how to work with a stock broker who knows his business.

By and large, the competence of a widow depends on the competence of her husband and the sort of business he was in. If a man owned a delicatessen and his wife helped him run it, obviously she doesn't need special training or preparation in order to maintain a steady flow of income for the family after he has passed on.

But most of us work for someone else, bring home a weekly or monthly paycheck, and try to build our widow's security through various devices like insurance programs, mutual fund investments, and the purchase of stocks and bonds.

Throughout America there has sprung up a great secondary market of investments. Insurance companies are secondary investors; so are mutual funds. They take your money, invest it for you, and pay you part of the earnings they get.

For some reason during the past 20 years, there has been a growing timidity among younger people to tackle the problem of investments first hand. A great many are afraid they'll lose money; some are even afraid they'll be gypped by Wall Street "operators." One of the reasons for this belief may be because it has been politically profitable for some to draw national attention to the few scoundrels who did business in Wall Street, and to ignore the thousands of investment and stock firms that maintain the highest level of ethics found anywhere in American business.

It has led to a mounting desire to have some second person—an insurance company or a mutual fund—do the investing.

Unless a man is so terrifically busy he can't spare the time to give the matter some thought, there's no reason why he shouldn't handle at least some of his own investments.

The same is true for his wife or his widow.

In a previous chapter we have noted how women are inheriting (or otherwise acquiring) an increasing amount of America's wealth, particularly invested wealth.

If we are to perpetuate the capitalistic system, if we are to maintain a steady and free flow of new wealth into new investments so that new enterprises can come into existence or old ones can expand, it is necessary that our wives know something about the function of the investment and securities market.

Wall Street does not operate on tips or inside information, the general belief notwithstanding.

The most successful investors are those who pay no heed to the dopesters but who are avid students of the passing scene. For the price of a newspaper, anyone can be as alert and as keenly aware as the most knowledgeable and most successful investor.

One of the few good talking points *against* insurance is inflation and resulting loss of purchasing power of the dollar. In other words, it's pure speculation on whether the dollars you're paying into insurance programs now will buy as much or only half as much 20 years from now.

It has been shown conclusively that money invested in most common stocks in 1935 has kept pace with inflation. The value of the stocks has increased at least as much as, and in many cases more than, the cost of living.

Any well-run family budget will include in it somewhere plans for an investment program, either for the present or the future.

If you have planned wisely, your widow will inherit some stocks when you die.

But even if you haven't, she will be inheriting, probably, a substantial sum of cash from your insurance and from other benefits you have acquired along the way. No matter what your station in life, the amount of money you will leave your widow will, if you're an average man, be more than she's accustomed to handle.

A man who earns $3,500 a year will generally leave an insurance policy larger than that. So will a man who earns $35,000 a year. And so on. So the assumption is that the widow will have in her hands, all at once, a generous (to her) sum of money.

What's she going to do with it?

Will she recognize the fact that even though she's rich right now, there'll be no further income unless she earns it herself or her money earns it for her? Will she buy that good coat she has always wanted— not a mink, necessarily, but a better one than she has had?

Or will she be thoroughly indoctrinated in the procedure she should follow?

Will she put aside enough to keep things going, pay up your bills and funeral expenses, and then take the rest to a good broker?

And once she has invested her money and is realizing some income from it, will she know how to trade on the securities exchanges? Will she know when to buy more stock, or when to sell the stocks she holds, so that she can make her investment grow and prosper?

It doesn't take a formal education to be a clever investor. Some of the most successful men on Wall Street did not have extensive educational preparation for the careers that have rewarded them so bountifully.

The "education" costs a few pennies a day—in the daily newspapers.

It is necessary to know only a few facts: that a stock is a share in a corporation and you can own it as long as you want and "share" in the earnings and profits of the corporation; that a bond is a mortgage on a corporation or city or county or state, and that a specified amount of interest will be paid until a specified date at which time the bond will be redeemed, just as a mortgage is one day paid off; that Wall Street is not the alpha and omega of all corporations, and is, in fact, more the tail of the dog than anything else; that what makes a stock of more value is the earnings potential of the corporation; that the earnings of a corporation are tied directly to sales, to costs, to taxes, and to capacity to produce efficiently; that profits grow and flourish only in a proper economic climate.

These are the things to remember. Thus, of primary importance is the political and economic health of the nation; of secondary importance is the health, efficiency, progressiveness, and foresightedness of a corporation; of least importance is what the traders are doing with the stock on Wall Street.

It was Bernard Baruch, I think, who said the best

way to make money in the stock market is to buy stock when it's low and sell it when it's high. Most persons thought he was being facetious. He wasn't. You have to know when to buy, but that's only half the trick; you have to know when to sell.

This information is at hand every day, any day. By reading daily newspapers it's possible to tell with a fair amount of accuracy the status of the nation's economic health, the condition of a certain corporation, and what the traders are doing with any corporation's stock in Wall Street.

In general a woman has a more meticulous mind than a man. It will be rewarding and enlightening to a husband if he tries to interest his wife in the business-economic-financial news of the world and attempts to relate it to her own security. As soon as she gets the gist of it, as soon as she realizes her comfort and security are involved, she'll grasp the whole general idea with amazing alacrity.

She'll soon know that the tax bill being wrangled in Congress can mean a deal more than just the extent of the personal income tax she'll pay next year. It won't take long for her to know that there's a tremendous amount of significance in such dull statistical information as retail sales; carloadings; steel production; electric production; food consumption; the price of cotton and the price of hogs.

If she owns two shares of Gimbel Brothers stock, she'll worry not alone about retail sales. She'll be concerned about the rate of personal income, the amount of savings in banks, the prospect of higher freight rates, the worry that wool prices might fall, leaving Gimbel's with a costly inventory of suits while other suits are being manufactured at lower price; the rumors of another round of wage increases for sales personnel.

In short she'll be an interested reader of the daily press. She'll also be a competent business woman, whether she knows it or not.

Before my wife and I had money enough to invest, we used to "make believe" invest. We'd study the papers for a couple of weeks and decide, perhaps, that we'd like to buy some utility stocks because the utility companies were going to make some money on their new natural gas pipelines running from Texas and Pennsylvania to the North and Northeast. Then we'd "invest" a few dollars on some selected utility stocks, writing ourselves little certificates. In a few weeks or months we'd know whether it had been wise. We learned by trial and error without risking a cent.

We have always liked to consider our savings account merely a temporary depository for future investments. Of course, we like to leave a reasonable amount in our savings account for contingencies, but whenever we can accumulate enough extra money in the savings account, it goes into carefully selected securities in the stock market.

With my broker, senior partner in a large New York brokerage house, I have prepared three sample investment "portfolios" for women. They are particularly devised for women and do not include "speculative" stocks, though they contain some that were believed, at the time the lists were prepared, to have a growth potential.

In no respect may this be considered the private

list of a couple of insiders who have had some good tips. By the time you read this, some of these stocks may not be such good investments after all. These are merely representative stocks and are designed to show how a widow can get a return from investments of insurance (or other) money in sums of $10,000, $25,000, and $50,000.

For the sake of hazarding a bet, however, I'd make a moderate wager at the time of this writing that a year—or two years from now—these lists will be standing up pretty well.

In the selection of the individual issues for these three widows' lists, we have tried to stress essentially "defensive" securities. This is a Wall Street term which means they are usually unassailable by fluctuations in the economy and are designed to protect the preservation of capital and to maintain regular dividend income.

It can be seen at a glance that each portfolio will yield something like 6 per cent on the investment.

All the companies represented in these lists are leaders in their respective industrial fields and are uniformly characterized by strong financial positions, good earnings, and records of unbroken dividend payments over a long period of years.

Since the dividend rates appear well protected by earnings of the various corporations, the annual income returns on the portfolios seem secure.

The market action of the 25 common stocks in the following lists has shown above-average stability. Although there has occasionally been a wide fluctuation in some of these stocks, it seems unlikely that a widow will find that the market prices have fallen

Suggested List for Investment of $10,000 by a Widow

Issue	Number of Shares	Current Market Price	Current Market Value	Estimated Dividend Rate	Estimated Dividend Income	Yield	Dividends Paid Since
American Natural Gas	60	32	$1,920	$1.80	$108	5.63%	1904
American Telephone & Telegraph	14	154	2,156	9.00	126	5.84	1881
Sunshine Biscuit	30	65	1,950	4.00	120	6.15	1927
Union Tank Car	50	40	2,000	2.60	130	6.50	1914
Universal Leaf Tobacco	80	25	2,000	1.70	136	6.80	1927
Total			$10,026		$620	6.18%	

Suggested List for Investment of $25,000 by a Widow

Issue	Number of Shares	Current Market Price	Current Market Value	Estimated Dividend Rate	Estimated Dividend Income	Yield	Dividends Paid Since
Chesebrough Mfg.	37	70	$2,520	$4.25	$153	6.07%	1883
Commonwealth Edison	80	32	2,560	1.80	144	5.63	1890
Electric Storage Battery	60	42	2,520	2.50	150	5.95	1901
International Harvester	80	33	2,640	2.00	160	6.06	1910
Norfolk & Western Ry.	50	50	2,500	3.50	175	7.00	1901
Pacific Lighting	50	51	2,550	3.00	150	5.88	1909
Public Service Electric & Gas	100	26	2,600	1.60	160	6.15	1906
Standard Oil of N. J.	30	80	2,400	4.50	135	5.63	1882
Underwood Corp.	50	52	2,600	4.00	200	7.69	1911
Union Pacific	20	115	2,300	6.00	120	5.22	1900
Total			$25,190		$1,547	6.14%	

Suggested List for Investment of $50,000 by a Widow

Issue	Number of Shares	Current Market Price	Current Market Value	Estimated Dividend Rate	Estimated Dividend Income	Yield	Dividends Paid Since
American Home Products	130	39	$5,070	$2.20	$286	5.64%	1919
Beneficial Loan	150	34	5,100	2.00	300	5.88	1929
Consumers Power	130	36	4,680	2.00	260	5.56	1913
Detroit Edison	210	23	4,830	1.40	294	6.09	1909
H. L. Green	130	39	5,070	2.50	325	6.41	1935*
National Dairy Prods.	90	54	4,860	3.00	270	5.56	1924
Reynolds Tob. B.	140	35	4,900	2.00	280	5.71	1918
Scovill Mfg.	160	32	5,120	2.00	320	6.25	1856
Sutherland Paper	240	24	5,760	1.50	360	6.25	1923
Texas Gulf Sulphur	40	113	4,520	7.00	280	6.19	1921
Total			$49,910		$2,975	5.96%	

* Company incorporated in 1932.

and her $25,000 (or $10,000 or $50,000) investment has dropped off.

She should not have to pump additional money into her portfolio to maintain an even income. And, should she have to sell some of her stock to raise money for some unexpected emergency, she should not have to take a severe capital loss because the value of the stock has decreased. On the contrary, there is the prospect that some of these stocks will increase in value, though none of them, in any respect, may be considered as "speculative" issues—that is, those that might plunge ahead to new highs.

There are several "growth" stocks in these portfolios, stocks which, the experts believe, will increase in value. Among those considered to have growth potentials, either in the near future or over a longer period of time are American Natural Gas, Public Service Electric & Gas, Standard Oil (New Jersey), Union Pacific, Beneficial Loan, National Dairy Products, and Texas Gulf Sulphur.

It may be seen from the foregoing lists of securities, that a widow who invests $10,026 will receive a dividend yield of $620 annually, or 6.18 per cent on her investment. In very few other places could she get such a high return on her money with such small risk. There is the likelihood, too, that the value of some of these securities will increase. American Natural Gas, for instance, faces an interesting future as pipelines are expanded to bring natural gas to far regions of the country. She could, if values increase, sell some of her stock, take the profit, and still keep about $10,000 invested.

That is true, of course, with the other two portfolios as well.

You will note, in looking over these stocks selected by Reynolds & Company, that some of the corporations have paid dividends consistently as far back as the early 1880's. The most recent dividend record is for H. L. Green, starting in 1935. But that company wasn't incorporated until 1932.

A young man starting out in life might think that it's unlikely he will ever have as much as $10,000 to invest at one time. If he thinks about his widow's chances for investing that amount, he'll soon realize that it's quite possible she might be handling $10,000 or more in an investment program.

If a young man starts early enough he can get $20,000 worth of life insurance at a very reasonable price—say $400 or $500 annually. If, after 20 years of married life, during which time he has managed to pay off the mortgage on his home, his wife becomes a widow and is paid the $20,000 by the insurance companies, there is no reason why she cannot invest $10,000 of it, or even $15,000, keeping the balance to live on until dividend checks start coming in.

In these sample portfolios we have not dealt with shares in mutual funds, though stock in mutual funds is currently very popular. Many investment companies of this type have had extremely interesting growths during the past few years and investments in their securities have proved, in the main, to be sound and wise.

It is possible to buy shares of investment companies or mutual funds on the installment basis, pay-

ing so much a month over a period of years, and the
earnings start accumulating soon after one joins the
plan.

In its simplest form, a mutual fund works this way:
the money you, and presumably thousands of others,
send each month is invested in one monstrous portfolio of securities. The earnings from the portfolio
are divided among the mutual fund owners according to the size of the individual's interest, or investment, in the fund.

I can think of no easier way to become an investor
and to share in the profits accruing from America's
miraculous industrial growth. For as little as $5 or
$10 a month invested in a mutual fund, one can be-
come the joint owner of the shares of the republic's
most thriving corporations. There is relatively little
risk, too, for these funds are invested and managed
by experts who are wary of each waver and fluctuation in the nation's economy.

Of course, one pays for this service. Costs of this
expert management are deducted from the yields and
profits of a mutual fund. But it's a good program for
the amateur investor.

The increasing patronage of mutual funds attests
to their soundness and popularity. Regular monthly
payments permit even the lowest bracket wage or
salary earner to participate in the growth of corporations as shareholders.

It is also possible to buy outright the shares of the
mutual funds themselves. Such shares are traded on
the stock exchanges and have fluctuating values, as
do the securities of other businesses and enterprises.

There are two kinds of mutual funds. The open end fund and the closed end fund. Open end funds are ready to add new members at any time. One may become a participant merely by agreeing to make regular payments or by purchasing the shares outright. Closed end funds start out with an initial subscription of stock. The revenue from the sale of securities is invested and the proceeds accumulate in the form of dividends to the shareholders. If the fund is managed wisely, the shares, when offered for resale in the exchanges, are of more value than when they were purchased.

I consider mutual funds to be good investments for widows. I also feel that it is a good idea for busy husbands to look into the possibilities of mutuals for they offer a reasonable and unusually safe means for participating in the stock market without requiring the constant supervision necessary when doing one's own buying and selling of securities. In short, it might be wise to let the professionals do your investing for you if you are too busy to do your own or feel that you do not know enough about general investments and the way the stock markets operate.

Insurance companies will render this service, in some respect, with retained benefits.

Chapter Seven

YOU CAN LEAVE HER A TRUST FUND

If a man leaves enough money, he can arrange to have it handled in trust by a bank or an individual. But most banks prefer not to work with small amounts—say, anything less than $25,000 or $30,000. It's not worth their while, for in some states they work on exceptionally low commissions.

Under the trust procedure, the trustee invests the money and pays the widow an income from earnings. This can be a stipulated yearly income, leaving the balance of earnings to accumulate and be reinvested, though this is not allowed in New York or Louisiana. A bank's trust department can do this for terms of the trust can be made to suit the convenience of the beneficiary. The bank can even be named as co-trustee. A broker must act on the instructions of his client, though he may, from time to time, give advice.

Banks in some states are expressly permitted by law to pool many trusts in one common trust fund, creating a form of mutual fund and the total is handled in one investment program.

Fact is, though, that the prudent man pays stiffer taxes all the way through life these days. His taxes are tougher as he earns more, and if he succeeds in accumulating enough, his survivors will be made to pay estate and inheritance taxes.

You can't take it with you, it's true. But you can't leave it all behind, either. Both the federal government and the state will want some of the accumulation of your lifetime.

As of fiscal year 1953, there's a specific federal exemption of $60,000 on estates, but any estate inventoried at greater than that (again, don't forget the value of those golf clubs) will get hit for a federal tax. It's 3 per cent on the first $5,000 over the exemption, 7 per cent on the next $5,000, and 11 per cent on the next $10,000. After that the taxes really bite so that there are two federal taxes on estates over $100,000.

Most states have an inheritance or an estate tax, but they are usually lower than those asked for by Uncle Sam. Even if there is not now a tax in your state, it must be considered a possibility, for new tax laws are always being devised.

The safest thing, if you see that the chips are rolling in comfortably, is to consult with the trust officer in your bank.

It is advisable, if the estate is likely to be a substantial one (anything in the neighborhood of $100,-000 is substantial to a trust officer) to name the bank as your trustee and executor of your estate.

Then you'll get expert advice on things which

your widow would be unable to handle alone. You'll get correct answers on whether or not to take the marital deduction allowed by law, what assets to sell to meet estate liabilities, how best to dispose of personal effects, how to handle your business interests, what to do with your real estate, including your home, how to handle your life insurance, what disposition to make of jointly held property. That is what is known as an estate planning job, and banks do not charge for it.

You will get the best possible advice on how and where to best provide for the tax burden you know will come; how much you should give to charity to keep the taxes within reason; and, perhaps most important, what to do with your portfolio of stocks and other securities.

Then, after your death, the bank can actually handle your securities, collect the income, and virtually assume the responsibility of providing for your wife's welfare.

In recent years there has been an increasing interest on the part of banks in small estate administration and in ways in which to effect savings in both time and money in the settlement of small estates.

However, under the standard statutory administration procedure, an estate in the lower brackets undergoes a shrinkage of as much as 15 to 20 per cent for administration costs alone and a minimum period of 6 to 12 months is required before the transfer of ownership to the heirs is completed.

Thus, since there is no special legislation for small estates, the widow and sole heir of a man who has died with nothing but an unimproved city lot worth $1000 can become a freeholder and taxpayer only after she has raised $150 to $200 for administration expenses (probably from the insurance he has left her) and even then, she must wait 6 months or longer for this privilege. If the time seems ripe to sell the property before that time, she may do so only by advancing an additional $35 to $50 or even more for costs of publication, citations, and extra legal expense.

Miscellaneous pieces of legislation have been drafted, somewhat hurriedly, in several states in recent years to take care of smaller estates. Some of them permit collection of such items as bank accounts, accrued wages, death benefits, and such without "supervision."

Probate laws in America have a long way to go. They are in no respect uniform, and in many cases are outmoded.

For instance, I can see no reason why, when an estate is being settled, the personal representative or executor cannot be privileged, at his or her option, to appear in person before the court in all matters relating to the estate under his administration, unless, of course, a will is being contested.

There is no reason why the probate courts cannot provide at cost printed forms of all documents required to be filed with the courts.

As it is now, probate courts in many states require that a lawyer be present. This, of course, adds to so-called "administration costs" and becomes a problem for the widow trying to settle a small estate.

The relationship between the trust departments of banks and the legal profession is rapidly improving, and out of the closer harmony, better, more equitable probate laws may develop for the benefit of the small-to-medium estates.

Chapter Eight

❡❡❡❡❡

WHAT SHE SHOULD KNOW
ABOUT FINANCE

Every human being, unless he is especially dedicated to some ideal which eschews the value of wealth, is "finance-minded" whether he realizes it or not.

But it's women, particularly housewives, who carry around a deep-seated appreciation of what happens to prices of retail goods and foodstuff when there are fluctuations in the republic's economy. It has always seemed strange to me that so few women follow the process through to the source; I have always wondered why more of them have not become top financial experts. Certainly the women who decide not to buy canned peas this week because they'll probably be lower in price next week could develop, without a great deal of effort, an ability to do similar evaluations on stocks. Or grain or cotton or tobacco.

It seems a waste of talent to apply the natural, intuitive, price-appraising abilities of women solely to the pennies involved in retail prices. Some of these same efforts, properly placed, could be devoted to *earning* money instead of just *saving* it.

After all, a good stock is merely a good bargain. Who's better qualified to identify a bargain and take advantage of it than a good housewife?

Finance has come of age in the past generation— but the past generation has not kept pace with finance. It is odd that so many millions of Americans deal with the subject of finance yet fail to realize that they're doing so. Very few Americans have refrained from making loud and serious comment on the subject of inflation. Few, indeed, are the citizens who have not wondered about the diminishing purchasing value of dollars in their insurance programs; who have not struggled to meet higher taxes; who have not squeezed the piggy bank to keep the mortgage payments current or to pay the monthly rent. Yet if you asked most of them if they knew anything about finance, they'd grin sheepishly and say it's a subject they've never learned much about.

Across the nation each morning, millions rush for newspapers to read of the happenings of the preceding 24 hours, never realizing that, exclusive of the sports news and funnies, most of the stories they read are concerned with finance or economics.

When we read of trouble in Iran, it's because of oil deposits and that concerns our gasoline and fuel oil. When we read of the establishment of the North Atlantic Treaty Organization, it's because of the economic compatibility—in fact, the economic interdependence—of the countries in the pact. We read of American loans to the British; of Britain's struggle to give back to private individuals the industries that were nationalized under socialism. We read of long wrangles in the American Senate over the payment of farm support prices, or of hot arguments in the House over plans to build more federal hydroelectric projects.

All this is finance. All of it affects prices. All of it concerns the economic climate in which business is operated, and that determines the size of profits. Profits, more than anything else, determine the size of dividends, and hence, the value of stock. And that affects you, and you, and you. . . .

It's really as simple as that.

But before anyone is really qualified to trade actively in the stock markets, he (or she) should know how to read the business barometers, the little items in the financial sections of newspapers which seem so dull, but which are loaded with such potential power.

The average person might find it hard to believe that such uninteresting statistics as Ward's weekly "Automotive Report" could contain a crystal ball. But there's one hidden therein. The plodding figures can show fairly accurately just how readily Americans are parting with their savings to buy new cars. It doesn't take much imagination to see what this means to banks (who will finance the cars), to the steel companies (who will provide steel for them), to the rubber companies (who will furnish the tires), to the textile companies (who will supply upholstery and tire fabric), and to thousands of other supplying industries.

A half-hour's daily reading in the financial section of a newspaper can give the reader a bushel basket full of crystal balls. One can virtually *feel* the ebb and flow of the economic tide by reading such tidbits as: bank clearings, building construction, business failures, carloadings, metals production, crop reports, petroleum production, department store sales, electric power production, employment, foreign trade, life insurance sales, paper production, railroad earnings, and the wholesale price index.

To instruct a wife in the intricacies of the stock market, a man should first teach her to appraise these regularly appearing news items, and to get the meat out of them.

Then she's ready to do business on Wall Street.

There's a lingo on Wall Street that's hard, at first, to understand, but like many dialects, it soon becomes easy. Brokers, in dealing with newcomers to the market, sometimes forget that such terms as "ex-dividend," or "cash sales" or "seller's option" or "Dow averages," may sound strange to the untutored, particularly women.

But for practical purposes, these terms will not be required for the casual or incidental trader, and, even if they are, they won't remain confusing very long.

By far the most popular statistical table in any newspaper is that carrying the lists traded on the two principal stock exchanges, the New York Stock Exchange and The American Exchange, formerly the

Curb Exchange. (The Curb Exchange, smaller of the two, derived its former name from its traditions: about 25 years ago many of the transactions were conducted on the sidewalk.)

On page 82 is a reproduction of a portion of the table of stocks on the New York Stock Exchange carried in a recent edition of the New York *Herald Tribune.*

The stock for American Telephone & Telegraph Company, most widely held American corporation (there are over 1,000,000 stockholders), is encircled.

Note that it is abbreviated to "Am Tel&Tel" so that all pertinent information can be contained in one line of type.

Looking far to the right, in the next-to-the-last column of figures, you can see that its closing price the preceding afternoon was $157¾ (or $157.75 a share) up ¾ of a point (last column) from the day's low.

Up at the very top of the listing appears the legend of what is printed below. It can be seen that the first two figures are the high and low for the year. Thus AT&T'S high was 161⅜ and its low, 150⅞ per share. The figure "9" appearing after the name of the stock in AT&T stands for the annual dividend which has been paid, $9 per share. The "111" represents the sales. Referring back to the top of the column, it is seen that sales are in 100's, so that the daily turnover in telephone stock was 11,000 shares. Next in order appear the opening price, the high for the day, the low for the day, the closing price, and the net change.

By looking over the plus and minus signs in these

The New York Stock Exchange

Monday, Dec. 22, 1952

Record of Stock Market Trend

1952 High	Low	Stock and div in $	Sales in 100s	Open	High	Low	Close	Net chg.
64¼	41¾	Abbott L 1.80a	16	45	45¾	45	45¾	+ ¾
125	108	Abbott L pf 4	1	111	111	111	111	+ ½
8⅝	5⅝	ACF Brill	19	6⅛	6⅛	6	6⅛	+ ⅛
30⅛	24¾	Acme Stl 1.60	2	25⅜	25⅜	25⅜	25⅜	....
35⅜	30⅝	AdamsExp 2.40e	5	33¼	33¾	33¼	33¾	+ ½
42¼	33¾	Adams Millis 2e	1	34½	34½	34½	34½	− ¼
64	56	Addressog 3b	1	56	56	56	56	....
32¾	24¾	Admiral 1	35	31	31⅜	30½	30½	− 3⅝
9⅜	7⅞	Affil G Eq .40	13	9	9⅛	9	9	....
29⅝	24	Air Reduc 1.40	30	29⅝	29⅝	28⅞	28⅞	− ⅝
115½	106½	Air Red pf 4½	1	114½	114½	114½	114½	+ ½
3⅜	2¾	Alaska Jun	5	2¾	2⅞	2¾	2⅞	....
23¾	18¼	Aldens 1½	5	19⅜	19⅜	19⅜	19⅜	− ⅛
5¼	2¾	Alleghany	257	5⅛	5¼	5	5⅛	− ⅛
158	79⅜	Alleg pf	5	153½	158	153½	158	+4½
46⅞	31⅞	Alleg L Stl 2b	17	36⅞	36⅞	36⅛	36⅛	− ½
9¾	8	Allen Ind .80	2	9¾	9¾	9¾	3¾	+ ⅛
78⅜	67¼	Allied Ch 2.40a	12	75	75½	74¾	74¾	− ¼
21½	18	Allied Kid 1.60	1	19½	19½	19½	19½	....
36	32½	Allied Mills 2a	1	32⅞	32⅞	32⅞	32⅞	....
40⅝	36	Allied Strs 3	15	38⅞	38⅞	38⅜	38⅜	− ⅜
61¼	46¼	Allis Chal 4	63	60⅞	61¼	60¼	61¼	+ ¾
122	95⅜	Allis Ch pf 3¼	2	121	122	121	122	+1½
48	36¼	AlphaP Cem 3e	1	46½	46½	46½	46½	....
54½	47¾	Alum Ltd 2	3	52⅜	52¾	52⅜	52½	− ¼
97	73¼	Alum Co Am 3	22	94	97	94	97	+3½
3⅛	2⅛	Amal Lea	6	2½	2½	2⅜	2⅜	− ⅛
235	141½	AmeradaPet 2a	30	193	193	191	191½	−1½
70¾	60¼	Am Ag Ch 3a	5	69¼	70	69¼	70	+2
16⅜	12¼	Am Airlines ½e	57	14¾	14⅞	14⅝	14¾	− ¼
90	73	Am Airl pf 3½	8	79¼	80	79	80	....
19½	16⅝	Am Bk Note 1	7	18⅝	18⅝	18⅝	18⅝	....
61½	55	†Am Bk N pf 3.z	400	56⅛	56⅛	55½	56	....
15⅜	10⅝	Am Bosch .90r	67	10¾	10⅞	10¾	10¾	....
53¼	43	Am Bos pf 2¾	1	43½	43½	43½	43½	− ¼
41¾	36⅝	Am Br Shoe 3	2	38¾	38¾	38	38	− ¼
107	102	Am Br Sh pf 4	1	103	103	103	103	....
12¾	8⅛	Am Brdcast	17	9⅝	9¾	9⅝	9¾	+ ¼
6	4¼	Am Cbl&R .15e	28	4½	4½	4¼	4½	+ ¼
36⅛	28⅛	Am Can 1.40	28	35¾	36	35⅝	35⅞	− ⅛
45½	32½	Am Can pf 1¾	2	43⅞	43⅞	43⅝	43⅝	....
42⅞	31	Am Car&F 3b	7	37⅛	37⅛	36¾	36¾	− ¼
83½	73½	AmCar&F pf 7	1	78½	78½	78½	78½	+ ½
50⅞	42⅜	Am Chicle 2a	15	46½	47¼	46½	47⅝	+ ⅛
19⅜	14¾	Am Col 1.10e	12	16¾	16¾	16½	16½	− ½
26	20⅝	Am Cry S 1.20a	5	21¾	22⅜	21¾	22⅜	+ ½
96½	89	†AmCryS pf4½	z20	91	91	90	90	−2
59¾	50⅝	Am Cyan 1h	70	53⅝	54	53½	53½	− ¼
54½	33⅞	Am Distill 2	6	37⅜	37½	37⅜	37½	+ ½
7¾	6	Am Enc T ½e	7	7⅝	7¾	7½	7½	+ ⅛
33½	29¾	Am Eur 2.80e	2	31	31	31	31	+ ⅞
18¼	16⅛	Am Export 1½	14	16¼	16¼	16⅛	16¼	+ ⅛
12½	7¾	Am&F Pw .10r	133	8⅞	8⅞	8¾	8¾	− ⅛
66⅝	58	Am Gas&El 3b	14	66¼	66⅝	65⅞	65⅞	....
55	45⅝	Am Haw SS 3	5	51	51	50½	50½	− ⅛
161⅜	150⅞	Am Tel&Tel 9	63	157¼	157¾	157¼	157¾	+ ¾
66⅞	54⅞	Am Tob 3a	64	66	66	65¼	65⅝	− ⅛

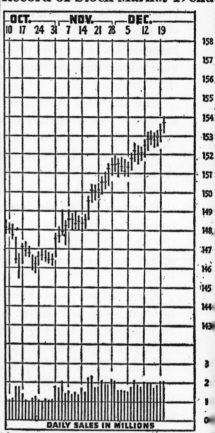

High, low and closing prices of New York Herald Tribune's 100-stock averages

columns, one can have a fairly accurate appraisal of the state of American business.

Looking over the rest of the list you may see small symbols appearing after the name of the stock or after the figure for its current dividend. These symbols are used merely to keep the list uncluttered. At the end of the stock list each day is printed a key to the signs and footnotes (see page 82).

The very first stock, Abbott Laboratories, carries the letter "a" after its dividend of $1.80. Looking to the key of symbols, one learns that this symbol "a" means there is also an extra dividend, or even more than one.

To get back to those bewildering terms used by the Wall Street fraternity, here are a few you may come in contact with:

Cash Sales	*Under the Rule*
Market Averages	*Seller's Option*
Most Active List	*Odd Lot Trading*
Ex-Dividend	*Premium Rates*
Street Names	*Puts and Calls*

And here's what they mean:

Cash Sales. This has to do with the delivery date of stocks. When shares are bought in the conventional manner, the broker must deliver them to the buyer by 12 noon on the third full business day following the sale. Should the buyer want immediate delivery, he would buy for cash. The broker would be making a "cash sale." These are very prevalent at year's end when cash sales are advantageous for tax purposes.

Market Averages. Are averages of a selected number of stocks in selected groups. The New York *Herald Tribune's* stock average is based on 100 representative issues to keep a record of progress of the stock market and the general tone of the financial community.

Most Active List. Is a list of the 15 most active stocks on the New York Stock Exchange, the 5 most active domestic stocks on the American Exchange, and the 5 most active foreign stocks on the American.

Ex-Dividend. Is a symbol carried in stock lists to indicate that a dividend is to be paid by a corporation but that the time for purchasing the stock in order to get the dividend has passed. A corporation usually declares a dividend payable on a certain date to shareholders of record on a particular date. Say, for instance, payble on September 1 to holders of record August 5. Two full business days before August 5 (because of the length of time it takes to deliver a share of stock), the stock is listed as "ex-dividend" by the stock exchange. It will so remain until the date of payment.

Street Names. Not all stock certificates are held by their owners. Sometimes buyers of shares prefer to have them held by their brokers. Thus when dividends are declared, the check is not sent to the rightful owner, but to the broker or to a "Street Name." Such practices were more prevalent when margin trading was more popular.

Under the Rule. If, for any reason, the seller of securities is unable to deliver the certificates to the buyer, he may be brought in "under the rule." The rule is that the stock may be bought at the market for immediate delivery to the purchaser, the bill being paid by the seller.

Seller's Option. If a seller is unable to deliver his stock to the purchaser in the normal length of time (if, for instance, his certificates are in a safe-deposit box many miles away), he may offer the stock for sale with a "seller's option," which usually carries with it some concession in price.

Odd Lots. Most stocks are traded in lots of 100 shares each. When a stock is inactive for a considerable length of time, the lots are sometimes reduced to 10 shares by the Exchange. Whenever a customer wishes to buy or sell less than 100 shares of any given stock, he is buying or selling in "odd lots."

Premium Rates. When a trader is "short" of stocks —that is, he has committed himself to deliver a specified number of shares of a certain stock at a certain date—he borrows shares from other traders. If the stock is very active or there is substantial "short interest," it may be hard to borrow, and the lender can charge a premium rate.

Puts and Calls. The market in puts and calls is an operation of options, by a group of dealers with their own house rules. Here's how it works: If you think the stock of YXZ corporation, now selling at 100, is going to drop, you can buy a "put" on the stock which will entitle you, within a specified length of time (60 days or 90, or as high as 180 days) to "put" 100 shares of XYZ stock to the writer of the option at, say, 97. If, in the meantime, you've been able to buy the stock at 94, you've made a good profit. A "call" works just the opposite. If you think YXZ stock is going to go higher than 100, you might "call" on the writer of the option to deliver the stock at, say, 102. If it climbs to 105, you've realized a profit.

Chapter Nine

 ∈⊰⧓⊱∋

LEAVE HER SOME FINAL INSTRUCTIONS

It seems sensible to me to prepare a letter of final instructions and leave it with the other valuable papers where it will be found by your wife. Tell her about it, and let her know that you are covering such things as funeral arrangements, information about your business, and instructions on how to conduct her affairs.

This should not be morbid or sentimental. It is a business document, addressed to the most important business partner of your life. Give her the essential, practical details: how you want your funeral handled; whether you have paid for a cemetery lot; how and where to collect the life insurance; what she should do about any property you might own or any stocks or other investments you might have.

In preparing the letter, consider the many things she should know. Will she know where to bury you?

Have you selected an undertaker? Does she know all about your insurance? Have you told her about your stocks and other investments, and what details should she know about them?

Does she know the names of your banker, your lawyer, your broker?

What will she need to know about estate taxes and other taxes she may be required to pay?

What do you want to tell her about a budget tailored to her new income?

My own wife will get a letter something like this:

Darling:

As you know, we own a small lot in the cemetery in Connecticut. Though it's quite far from here, where we have spent so many happy years, I think it wise for me to be buried there, and you, too, when the time comes.

Because we have never been to church much here, I think it is best to have brief services in a funeral chapel here, and then hold brief services at the church in Connecticut, for that is where most of our relatives live.

Now about money matters. I have tried to arrange things so you can handle them easily. There is a will in the office of Bill Evans, our lawyer, and he will handle everything for you. The will leaves everything to you, and names you executor of my estate. That means that you can sell anything you want, if it is necessary to get cash.

The money you receive from my insurance may be the most we have ever had at one time. Don't let it throw you. The policies are in the safe-deposit box, but the policy numbers, names of the companies, and amounts of the policies are listed in that brown envelope marked "Insurance" in the strongbox.

I had a Mutual Fund program in the XYZ Fund. I sort of figured that the fund money would help put the children through college. Now they'll have to work too, of course, but there's no reason why they can't go to good schools. So why don't you leave the money in the fund and collect the dividends until you need the capital for the boys' education? You will know best about this, as time goes on.

There may be a tax on the estate. Don't worry, they'll let you know; but make sure Bill Evans knows, too, just so they won't put anything over on you.

You're going to have to cut down on everything. If you were to try to maintain payments on the mortgage here, it would eat up your insurance money. I own five-eighths of the house in Connecticut, you know; my brother owns the rest. I'd suggest that you sell my share and use the money to pay off the mortgage here. Or else sell this house and use the money to buy the other three-eighths of the house in Connecticut from my brother.

There will be some income from the stocks I have invested. All my stocks are in the safe-deposit box, but you'd better check, too, in the strongbox at home, just to make sure I haven't some recent certificates which I haven't put in the safe-deposit box. Our brokers, as you know, are Jones & Co., on Broadway, and the fellows I always talked to there are Jim Staley and Josh Harris.

I always kept about 15 per cent of our investments in speculative stocks. I figure you've got to be able to lose money as well as make it, if you're going to play with speculative stocks, so they may advise you to transfer that 15 per cent into safer securities. I have taught you how to read the stock market reports and how to watch the financial pages for developments in business, industrial, and economic news. Since this stock is your responsibility now, keep your eyes open!

After you decide about the house and have paid off the mortgage, either here or in Connecticut, settle down to a strict schedule on the amount of money you spend. Work out a budget and stick to it. That way, you can be comfortable, safe, and snug for years.

You will have a good deal of money that isn't "working." Don't listen to any investment schemes unless you first consult Bill or my brother Norm. You know the stories about how people connive to get the insurance money away from widows!

So that's it, darling. We've worked it out quite carefully, though there are, of course, flaws to our plans, for we don't know what lies ahead. I'm glad we had the good sense to think and talk about this. We planned it together, and *our* plan will go on working now that I've gone. Perhaps it will prove to be, as Elizabeth Barrett Browning suggested in her sonnet, that "if God choose, I shall but love thee better after death.". . .

Chapter Ten

ᏒᎷᎪᎷᏋ

HOW TO TEACH YOUR WIFE
TO BE A WIDOW

If the prospect of widowhood is approached sensibly
by a young married couple, it can buy a lot of comfort and peaceful sleep for both husband and wife
and may, in the end, contribute substantially to a
longer life for the husband. Few things are more
destructive of physical health than worry and nervous
tension.

A husband should undertake the job of instructing
his wife how to be self-sustaining just as soon as he
can, though it's never too late to begin.

A man who tackles the task with any amount of
enthusiasm will think of numerous more angles as
he goes along. For instance, I think it's a good idea
to have your wife meet your banker and get to know
him, as an individual and as your counselor on
money matters. Most wives, you know, think of bank-

ers as the flint-hearted ogres who turned thumbs down on her precious hubby's application for a measly $500 loan to buy carpeting for the living room just because he had three unpaid notes.

The same holds true for your lawyer, your broker, and, if you're rich enough to set up a trust, the trust officer in your bank.

Then, should the day arrive when she has to consult these men on matters vital to her livelihood and existence, she won't be dealing with strangers. She'll be at ease and more receptive to their expert advice.

Every wife is different—so I'm told. Each husband and wife will have to map out their own program, their own method of instruction, their own system of indoctrination.

But I do think there are eight vital steps which cannot be ignored or circumvented.

These are:

Teach her to handle budget matters, to write checks, to plan the family spending programs.

Prepare her for some gainful occupation so that she could, if necessary, be self-supporting.

See that she understands stocks and the stock market, and how to plan investments, for even if you don't own stocks, she may have to—or want to—invest your insurance money.

Make sure she gets to know your banker, your broker, your insurance man, and your lawyer.

And then to give her the tools to work with:

Prepare a will. Instruct her on how to be executor of your estate.

Stretch your insurance to cover the mortgage on your home, so she'll have it free and clear.

Keep some emergency money in her own private savings or checking account—in preference to a joint checking account.

Write her a letter, instructing her on what to do and what not to do, whom to talk to, how to handle the family affairs all alone.